To Johanna

Valentines Day 2002

Love
Dad

THE BOOK OF
LOVE

THE BOOK OF
LOVE

Romantic ways to create pleasure and harmony

CYNTHIA BLANCHE

Contents

Introduction

We are the dupes of myth when we upbraid
Ourselves because we love, for we are made
For loving: all the sweets of living are
For those that love. Be joyful, unafraid!

Omar Khayyám, *The Rubáiyat of Omar Khayyám*

Being truly in love is the most intoxicating experience you can have. There is no drug — natural or synthetic, legal or illegal — no thrill-seeking experience, that can summon from within you such a feeling of well-being, energy, and awareness of the essence of you.

There is no age limit when it comes to falling in love. The intensity can be just as great at 75 as it is at 15 or 25. Nor does that depth of feeling have to fade when the honeymoon is over or with time. You can be in a committed relationship without falling into the traps of repetition and routine. Maintaining the feeling of being in love, or reigniting it, can be sensuous, fun, and awakening. What's more, it's easy — you just need to know a few simple techniques.

This book shows you some of the ways in which you can experience "being in love" for the rest of your life. With help from your imagination, you can use these tips and suggestions as a springboard for inventing your own special rituals and experiences. The desire to give, being willing to receive, and some trust in your partner is all you need to begin.

And if you have recently parted from the one you love, this book provides some suggestions for comforting yourself. These will help counter any negative legacies and will prepare you for some new experiences.

Tensions from overwork or from financial problems can often overflow into our relationships. It can then be very difficult keeping love on track. Blame and recriminations not only create immediate crises, but they fester beneath the surface, ready to reemerge at the slightest opportunity.

How much better it would be to take your tensions to the aromabath together, to soak while listening to music by candlelight, breathe in the healing scents, and talk over your problems in the tub. Follow this with massage and your problems will take on new and manageable proportions — they will then take their proper distance to be finally dealt with at a more appropriate time.

There are many ways to dispel negative energies from your love life. The Chinese use the techniques of feng shui to ensure that the chi — life energy — flows, enriching, healing, and energizing heaven, earth, and humans. Some cultures use love spells and potions, while others have special rituals involving precious essential oils.

Crystals have energies that can be harnessed to dispel fear of relationships and negativity, and to strengthen your ability to give and receive love. Color and music have powerful vibrations that you can use to your advantage. And flowers and food elicit sensual feelings and generous inclinations.

Love is the greatest of all things, romantic love is but one aspect. Parents fall in love with their children, babies with their parents. There is love between friends, love for humanity, love for all things. People have sacrificed their lives for love, and it is not uncommon for a stranger to sacrifice his or her life for another. And to complete this volume of love are the stories of two great romances.

Love is what connects us to the universe and to one another. Love needs to be nurtured in all its forms; it should never be ignored and should always be appreciated.

"The average man is more interested in a woman who is interested in him than he is in a woman — any woman — with beautiful legs."
Marlene Dietrich

Flirting and Other Skills

Flirtation, attention without intention.

Max O'Rell, *John Bull and His Island*

Flirting is great fun. It is also normal, is not demeaning, and is probably biologically prompted. Both men and women do it. When you meet someone you are attracted to, flirting happens at an almost unconscious level, and this is the best way. You can deliberately flirt, but be aware of the difference between skilled flirting and the trying-too-hard, desperation variety.

So what is flirting? Flirting involves being totally focused on someone — being interested in their opinions, laughing at their jokes, making them feel attractive, interesting, and exciting. Eye contact is the most important aspect — hold that gaze just a little longer than you normally would, but with soft eyes and not for too long, as staring can be intimidating.

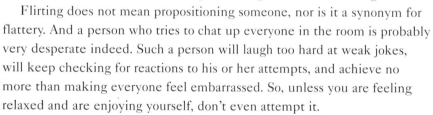

Flirting does not mean propositioning someone, nor is it a synonym for flattery. And a person who tries to chat up everyone in the room is probably very desperate indeed. Such a person will laugh too hard at weak jokes, will keep checking for reactions to his or her attempts, and achieve no more than making everyone feel embarrassed. So, unless you are feeling relaxed and are enjoying yourself, don't even attempt it.

When someone flirts with you, you will feel attractive and interesting. You do not have to be physically attracted to someone who flirts with you to like him or her. You do not have to be physically attracted to someone to flirt with that person. It is about making someone feel good, about bringing out the best in the person you're talking with.

You won't necessarily find the lover of your dreams by flirting, but if you refine the art of flirting, you will appear attractive and generous to the world at large — and that can only be good.

Attracting Love

Everyone knows someone who could be described as physically ugly but who is enormously attractive to the opposite sex. These people are always wonderful to be with, have a lightness of personality and wit, yet can get "deep and meaningful" at precisely the right time. On the other hand, there are some people whose extreme physical beauty seems to disappear when they open their mouths.

"It's what you are on the inside that counts" seems to be a cliché, and it is when tossed off without explanation. The trouble is that telling this to an insecure person is not going to help his or her confidence very much. What will help is the understanding that the way you think affects the way you are perceived by others; looks don't count. Both men and women want a partner who loves and understands them — and this has nothing to do with body shape or weight. But it does have a lot to do with personality and a person's ability to care and share.

The sexiest people have self-assurance. When your confidence level is not always playing on your mind, you have room to give the best of yourself to others. Self-absorbed people have space only for themselves, and self-absorption is always the result of lack of confidence — even in those people who seem to have everything.

Love is the poetry of the senses.
Honoré de Balzac, *The Physiology of Marriage*

Smile

Smiling people are popular people. Smiling suggests warmth and generosity. The impression given by someone who smiles easily is one of attractiveness, even if that person is not classically beautiful. Smiling will make you feel good; at the same time, everyone around you feels good, too. Even if you are not feeling happy, smiling can actually lift your mood — it may even make you feel carefree. A smile takes less effort than a frown; however, it is not enough to smile with the mouth alone. If you don't extend your smile to your eyes, stress will be placed on the muscles around your mouth, and you may be regarded as condescending or cold, distant, and aloof.

To feel the difference for yourself, try smiling just with your mouth. Now consciously involve your eyes. You will notice a distinct difference, not only in the shape your mouth makes but in the way you feel.

A Person Who is Attractive to be Around...

- smiles a lot

- laughs easily

- is interested in other people

- is a good listener

- doesn't look around the room while in conversation with someone

- has a relaxed presence

- doesn't dwell on his or her miseries and failures or boast about achievements

- doesn't get intense in inappropriate situations, i.e., when others are having a lighthearted get-together

- doesn't constantly interrupt

- is sympathetic to the problems of others

- has a sense of fun

Increasing Your Self-Confidence

You may think increasing your self-confidence is going to be difficult. In the beginning, you will have to use your will to overcome your fear — you will have to pretend to believe you will succeed. In the end, you will believe.

Ask yourself why you think others are more attractive to be around than you. Your answer could be: "People don't like me because I'm too boring/fat/thin/plain/beautiful..." The list can be endless.

Look at the box opposite to see what makes a person attractive to be around — none of these things are difficult for you to do. Your lack of confidence, your fear of being with others, will probably make you either tongue-tied or too talkative to begin with. The solution to this is easy. Everyone likes to talk about themselves. So let them. Until your confidence grows, let others talk and allow yourself to be the interested listener. Most people are interesting, and you can gain a lot of insight into people by simply asking questions and listening to their answers. Subjects to be avoided, unless they arise naturally and with someone with whom you feel an affinity, are: religion, politics, money, personal matters, and sex.

Lovers are fools, but nature makes them so.

Elbert Hubbard, *Epigrams*

> *If your love is unrequited, it means that the object of your desire is not your soul mate — but someone else out there is.*

Ways To Make You Feel and Be Attractive

• Always take care with your personal appearance. It tells the world how you wish to be seen — and you never know when you are going to bump into the lover of your dreams.

• It doesn't matter whether you are fat or thin, or what shape you are. The primary erogenous zone is the brain, not the body. In fact, being perfect is perfectly boring. It's a person's flaws that make him or her interesting. Everyone is potentially attractive. Feel attractive and you are attractive.

• Wear sexy underwear. Others do not have to see it for it to make you feel sexy. And if you feel sexy, these are the energies you will exude.

• Take aromabaths by candlelight with music playing in the background. It will relax you as well as increase your body awareness in a positive way.

• Smile, not just with your mouth but with your whole face. Even if you are feeling miserable, smiling will help lighten your mood. It also encourages others into your sphere.

• Do daily relaxation exercises.

• Keep busy and be a little mysterious, i.e., don't tell all about yourself.

• Go out dancing. Dancing gives you a positive body awareness, teaches you to let your body relax, and stimulates your body's senses, and it's great for toning up your muscles. The music also exhilarates you, and how can you be depressed or feel unattractive when you are dancing?

• Be playful. Be open to new opportunities for fun and delight.

How to Open a Conversation

People at gatherings expect to meet new friends, so it is not being pushy to casually approach a group of people or someone else standing alone and introduce yourself — but do remember to smile. If you are at the buffet table, you can say: "Don't you think the food's great?" When the person responds, you can then ask: "How do you happen to know (the host)?" and this will probably open up the subject of the other person's work or hobby. It is important that you approach with a feeling of openness and friendliness. Be bright and warm and people will respond in the same manner. It is a risk going up to someone, but if you approach with a grim expression, looking down at your shoes, you will probably be received in equal measure.

To minimize the risk of rejection, try to sense who the friendly people are at a gathering, and which ones are superficial. Someone who is looking around the room constantly, rather than at the person he or she is talking with, is probably going to be a superficial character. A person who is laughing or smiling, whose body seems relaxed, will probably also be friendly and kind.

If you do happen to make a mistake and approach someone unkind, dismiss that person without another thought and approach someone more deserving of your company. Certainly, you must not allow the bad manners of one person to affect your self-esteem.

Don't forget that the person you are talking to could also be very shy. Reticence is often a sign of shyness and not a sense of superiority. If that is the case, he or she will probably be very grateful that you have made an effort to strike up a conversation.

Feeling Good About Being Single

A lot of people feel desperate when they're not in a relationship. They feel as though they've failed at life or that they aren't attractive enough. Neither of these things is true unless you make it so. Consider the following points:

• There's nothing wrong with you. It's better to be alone than with someone you don't like.

• If you feel inadequate or need someone to validate your existence, then you are not ready for a healthy relationship anyway. Try doing some self-discovery work, then, when you're ready, someone you really like will come your way.

• Potential partners shy away when they sense desperation in someone — and desperate vibrations are hard to disguise.

• If you feel undesirable, you will emit that energy. Don't feel sorry for yourself; instead take steps to become desirable — this book provides plenty of tips. Besides, you should realize that if you were that desperate, you would be in a relationship — if you were prepared to take just anyone.

• If there's no one on the scene, don't sit at home feeling useless and embarrassed by your single status. Do something with your life that will make you feel happy. Expand your skills, or take up something you've always wanted to do, and get on with your life.

• Realize that being single is a luxury you may not have for very much longer.

• Blind dates work for some people, but these are high-pressure situations. You are much more likely to meet Mr./Ms. Right when you least expect it, in the least likely situations — so stop worrying!

If Your Love Leaves You ...

DO DON'T

Accept that your beloved has become your ex. Realize that your time together is over and that it is nobody's fault, only a natural parting of ways.

Grieve — as hard as you can. Get it all out. Punch a pillow, stamp and stomp, cry and yell — in the wilderness or in the privacy of your own home to some heart-wrenching music.

Keep your dignity. In the street outside your former beloved's house is not the place to express your feelings. Talk them out with your best friend, your sister, brother, mother, or father. Keeping your dignity will help heal your pain, and you won't have cause for self-recrimination later.

Exercise strenuously — run, power-walk, or play squash or racquetball — to (a) rid yourself of anger, (b) maintain a positive body image, and (c) look great once you're ready to date again.

Search for reasons to explain your beloved's behavior or believe that he or she still loves you. It will only lead to more heartbreak.

Deny your feelings or bottle them up. If you do, you could find it difficult to express love and affection in your next relationship, and the next, until you are able to deal with your feelings of grief and anger.

Fling yourself against the door or hold onto your love's leg to stop him or her from leaving your apartment. And don't stalk, don't even phone. Being pathetic is not going to encourage him or her to want you back. If you are meant to be together, your former partner will come back of his or her own free will.

Seek revenge. For the brief satisfaction this may give you, revenge will only continue your emotional upheaval and distress, and you will have a bitter outlook on life.

DO

DON'T

Pamper yourself. Indulge in beautiful things: aromabaths, essential-oil massages, beautiful music, good films, your favorite foods, your most attractive clothing. This treatment will counter any loss of confidence you might have suffered and keep you feeling good about yourself.

Wear colors that make you feel alive and vibrant. Taking care of your personal appearance is particularly important when you have had a blow to your confidence.

Smile, stand tall, walk with long strides, and hold your head high. You will feel better and people will respond with friendliness. This will aid you in your recovery and give you hope for the future.

Tell yourself that you will get over this and that there will be someone else for you down the road. This person will love you for yourself, and will regard your faults as nothing more than aspects of you.

Let your ex-lover's criticisms get to you. It was just his or her way of exerting control over you. If you even consider that he or she is right you could decide you're not good enough for anyone else. Besides, who is this person to criticize you?

Allow yourself to give in to feelings of unattractiveness. You will display this attitude to the world and some people might believe it.

Hang your head, stoop your shoulders, and walk slowly, dragging your feet. You will look years older than you are, and people will want to walk right on by.

Chant the mantra: "He/she was my soul mate, we were meant to be together. I'll never love anyone again." If the two of you really were meant to be together you would be.

Giving and Receiving Love

There is no remedy for love but to love more.

Henry D. Thoreau, *Journal,* **July 25, 1839**

The ability to both give and receive love is the most important aspect of a relationship. This is the kind of love that can withstand the worst problems life can throw at you. It will often mean giving way on a point of argument, or sacrificing a path or something you want, and it always means trusting your partner to have your best interests at heart.

When there is unlimited giving and receiving of love in a relationship, both of you know your best friend is always there to help you through times of stress and to share your moments of triumph. When you are sure of your partner's love, you know you don't have to feel defensive about your faults, because you know they are accepted as part of you. You don't ever have to wonder what your partner is up to when you're not around, nor do you need to be concerned if he or she is enjoying the company of an attractive person at a party. When there is a lot of love between two people, the love seems to spill over to family, friends, and even to strangers. People who share this kind of love are joyful, and joyousness is infectious.

Before there can be the joy of shared love, there needs to be mutual trust and affection. But if you or your partner lacks trust, or has insufficient belief in the other's love, your relationship will begin to deteriorate. Believe in your partner, otherwise you take the risk of losing someone who might have been your soul mate.

No one worth possessing
Can be quite possessed.

Sara Teasdale, *Advice to a Girl*

Keeping Love Alive

Mystery and anticipation are the hallmarks of the beginning of a relationship. Your imagination is filled with wonderful pictures of your future together. A common declaration lovers make to each other is, "We'll grow old together," as they see themselves in loving embraces even into their nineties.

You can keep the romance alive. There are many elderly couples who are just as romantic as they were when they were newly in love. But they didn't achieve this by sitting back and leaving it to fate — they never stopped thinking of themselves as lovers.

Lovers love to give and to share the trivial as well as the big events in life. Lovers will fight dragons and walk over burning coals to make the other happy. Lovers thank God or the universe every day for having found each other. Lovers are proud of each other's achievements and are always supportive. Lovers want for each other everything that will bring happiness.

When a Relationship Gets Boring

Boredom is often the result of repetition of activity and not your partner's personality. If you once found your partner fascinating, then you can again. Boredom will set in when you forget you are lovers, and this can happen easily when you are busy with work or family. Use the hints in this book and a little imagination to put variety and excitement back into your lives.

Grow old along with me!
The best is yet to be,
The last of life, for which the first was made:
Our times are in his hand
Who saith, 'A whole I planned,
Youth shows but half; trust God: see all, nor be afraid!'

Robert Browning, from *Rabbi Ben Ezra*

Rekindling Desire

• Affection is the greatest aphrodisiac there is, but only if you show affection every day, at any time of the day, for no other reason than that you love each other.

• Don't expect great heights of passion all the time, year after year. It is normal for passions to ebb and flow, according to the stresses of life.

• Learn how to give each other massages.

• Use scented oils in massage and baths.

• Use essential oils in an aromatherapy burner or a potpourri pot to create an atmosphere of sensuality in your home.

• Go for walks every day, take a different route and discover new things — houses, trees, gardens, or whatever your neighborhood offers.

• Change your menus frequently and experiment in the kitchen together.

• Talk every day about ideas, gossip, feelings, and discuss anything that's bothering you, even if it's each other. Unresolved conflict destroys passion faster than anything else.

• Be playful. Do silly things together. Enjoy each other.

• Be open to each other's moods and be sympathetic when necessary, and avoid being judgmental.

• If you are too busy to spend time together, then make time. Build it into your schedules and stick to it. Most work crises can wait until morning.

• Say every day how much you love each other.

Minimize Misunderstandings

At the beginning of a relationship, you have high expectations for everlasting happiness. The very thought of you and your beloved sitting in silence night after night, month after month, year after year, in different chairs in front of the TV, seems impossible. That happens to other people, not to you. You believe there is so much love between you that nothing could rip you apart.

And there is no reason why anything should, as long as you understand that a relationship can succeed only if you both work hard at keeping the communication lines open, are prepared to compromise, and let your partner have his or her way sometimes, just for the heck of it.

The greatest threat to your shared happiness is a breakdown in communication. This usually happens slowly and subtly. It begins because you or your partner — or both — get defensive about something. You don't want to "give in" because it might make you seem weak. Perhaps you feel your rights as an individual are at stake.

Vulnerability, closeness, dependence, sharing, revealing secrets — these are the great joys of a relationship. Some people are afraid if they open themselves up to these things, their partners will take advantage of them.

This is where trust comes in. Without trust, you cannot have a truly worthwhile, loving relationship. Make a pact with each other to be supportive, not judgmental; to remember that all people have faults and to be tolerant of each other's; to listen with an open mind to each other's fears and phobias; to give and receive love and affection; to never withhold love as an expression of anger or fear, but to talk, discuss, and resolve. Misunderstandings rarely develop in an atmosphere of trust.

Keeping Communication Lines Open

The best way to solve problems in relationships is to talk about them, but at the right time. In the heat of anger is not the right time, so walk away. Talk at the beginning of the problem, before tempers flare. If you allow that moment to pass without resolving the conflict, agree to a period of time for you both to get some perspective on the issue.

• If you have a resentment or a problem and don't get it off your chest, you will drive it underground, where it will fester and come out in all kinds of unreasonable ways. Meanwhile, your poor partner has no idea what he or she has done wrong — mind reading is the province of psychics.

• Getting things off your chest can be a selfish exercise if it is not done with sensitivity to your partner's feelings. Always wait for the right time and place. And approach the issue with consideration for your partner's personality and usual reactions to difficult issues.

• Treat your partner with the same respect you want for yourself.

• Never yell — at least not at your partner. Control yourself, then go outside or into a soundproof room and yell and scream. Punch a pillow or kick a ball around until your tensions have been released.

• Sometimes people are in bad moods because of something that has happened during the day. If you automatically assume the bad mood is directed at you, you will get defensive. Feel out the situation, and either leave your partner alone for a while to get over the worst of it or ask what the problem is. Your partner's personality will determine how you treat this.

Be interested in each other's opinions and ideas.

Respect each other's individuality.

Always be appreciative of each other's qualities and say so.

Always be kind to and considerate of each other.

Leave the judging of faults to others.

Sort out your conflicts before going to bed.

Realize there'll always be something to discover about each other.

Never take your life together for granted.

Share your problems, knowing you will find love and support.

Respect each other's life decisions.

Be affectionate every day.

Try to spend loving time together every day.

Take up hobbies or activities you can do together.

Treat each day as a new day of courtship.

Tree of Love

Beautiful words of love can heal a lover's rift or seal a courtship. If you're not confident of your love letter writing skills, let the poets do it for you.

Shall I compare thee to a summer's day?
Thou art more lovely and more temperate:
Rough winds do shake the darling buds of May,
And summer's lease hath too short a date.
Sometimes too hot the eye of heaven shines,
And often is his gold complexion dimmed;
And every fair from fair sometime declines.
But thy eternal summer shall not fade.

William Shakespeare

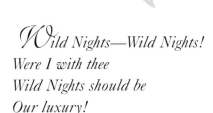

Wild Nights—Wild Nights!
Were I with thee
Wild Nights should be
Our luxury!

Futile—the Winds—
To a heart in port—
Done with the Compass—
Done with the Chart!

Rowing in Eden—
Ah! The Sea!
Might I but moor—Tonight—
In Thee!

Emily Dickinson

Come live with me and be my Love,
And we will all the pleasures prove
That hills and valleys, dale and field,
And all the craggy mountain yield.

There will we sit upon the rocks
And see the shepherds feed their flocks,
By shallow rivers, to whose falls
Melodious birds sing madrigals.

There will I make thee beds of roses
And a thousand fragrant posies,
A cap of flowers, and a kirtle
Embroidered all with leaves of myrtle.

A gown made of the finest wool,
Which from our pretty lambs we pull,
Fair linèd slippers for the cold,
With buckles of the purest gold.

A belt of straw and ivy buds
With coral clasps and amber studs:
And if these pleasures may thee move,
Come live with me and be my Love.

Thy silver dishes for thy meat
As precious as the gods do eat,
Shall on an ivory table be
Prepared each day for thee and me.

The shepherd swains shall dance and
sing
For thy delight each May-morning:
If these delights thy mind may move,
Then live with me and be my Love.

Christopher Marlowe

How do I love thee? Let me count the ways.
I love thee to the depth and breadth and height
My soul can reach, when feeling out of sight
For the ends of Being and ideal Grace.
I love thee to the level of every day's
Most quiet need, by sun and candlelight.
I love thee freely, as men strive for Right;
I love thee purely, as they turn from Praise.
I love thee with the passion put to use
In my old griefs, and with my childhood's faith.
I love thee with a love I seemed to lose
With my lost saints,—I love thee with the breath,
Smiles, tears, of all my life!—and, if God choose,
I shall but love thee better after death.

Elizabeth Barrett Browning

But were I loved, as I desire to be,
What is there in the great sphere of the earth,
And range of evil between death and birth,
That I should fear, — if I were loved by thee?
All the inner, all the outer world of pain
Clear Love would pierce and cleave, if thou wert mine,
As I have heard that, somewhere in the main,
Fresh-water springs come up thro' bitter brine.
'Twere joy, not fear, clasp'd hand-in-hand with thee,
To wait for death — mute — careless of all ills,
Apart upon a mountain, tho' the surge
Of some new deluge from a thousand hills
Flung leagues of roaring foam into the gorge
Below us, as far on as eye could see.

Alfred Lord Tennyson

Let me not to the marriage of true minds
Admit impediments. Love is not love
Which alters when it alteration finds,
or bends with the remover to remove;
O, no! it is an ever-fixed mark,
That looks on tempests and is never shaken;
it is the star to every wandering bark,
Whose worth's unknown, although his height be taken.
Love's not time's fool, though rosy lips and cheeks
Within his bending sickle's compass come;
Love alters not with his brief hours and weeks,
But bears it out even to the edge of doom.
       If this is error, and upon me prov'd,
          I never writ, nor man ever lov'd.

William Shakespeare

Taking the Stress Out of Romance

Diffidence and awkwardness are the two antidotes to love.

William Hazlitt, *Sketches and Essays*

Preparing for the Big Date

You are looking forward to going out with the person of your dreams. He or she is everything you've ever hoped for in a partner. And this is the first date! How thrilled you must be.

As the day progresses, excitement turns into apprehension.

This is the person you want more than anyone, and you really want to make a good impression. But you are so nervous that you are afraid you'll blow it by appearing inadequate, tongue-tied, unsophisticated, or boring.

Adrenalin is racing through your body, you are sweating, your nerves are on edge. How are you going to make a good impression in this state? How can you ensure that you'll be relaxed and as attractive as he or she obviously believes you are?

On the following pages is a routine for relaxation that begins early in the afternoon and continues right up until the time you go on your big date. It is a routine you will greatly enjoy and involves releasing tensions, calming the mind and body, and increasing your confidence and positive body awareness.

Run Those Demons Out

Run hard, and drive that apprehension out. Vigorous exercise is the best exorcist of pent-up tensions. Begin slowly, gradually increasing to a comfortable speed for distance. Or you may like to vary your speeds: Begin jogging, have a burst of hard running, slow to a jog, then when you feel you can, run hard again for a short time, before slowing to a jog. If you can keep this up for at least half an hour, an hour if possible, you will feel much less stressed than you did before setting out. You will probably even feel exhilarated and optimistic. An important point to remember with any hard exercise, is that you should warm up beforehand, and cool down afterward — never go directly from being stationary to hard exercise or from hard exercise to sitting on a chair. You could injure your muscles this way, causing spasms — you could also damage your heart.

Other good exercises for getting rid of tensions are tennis, long-distance cycling, aerobic exercises to music, and dancing.

Relaxation Routine

Try the routine on the following pages before your big date. It's a combination of exhilarating exercise and indulgent pampering and will leave you feeling vibrant and ready for anything.

1. Do some exercise. Go for a long run, or play a hard game or two of squash or racquetball, early in the afternoon.

2. Take a cool shower.

3. Do a deep relaxation session, see page 32.

4. Practice yoga positions, see pages 34–37.

5. Get a massage, see page 38.

6. Take an aromabath, see page 42.

7. Dress yourself in your most desirable clothing.

8. Greet your date with a big smile, and have a wonderful time.

Dance your way to harmony

Dancing is a great way to release tensions. It makes you feel happy, even euphoric. Be as creative as you like, and have fun. Don't regard it as an exercise, but as something you do to lift your spirits, giving you distance from your cares and worries. You make contact with your body when you dance. Move your arms and legs in flowing, creative ways, and feel your muscles and your skin and your energies flowing throughout your body.

Merging Mind and Body

It is important when you are about to go out on a big date that your nerves are calm and that you emanate a sense of self-assurance and wholeness of being. The following ritual helps center you, creating harmony and balance.

You can play soft music if you wish. Nocturnes by Chopin would be an excellent choice, since they are at the same time gentle, beautiful, passionate, and uplifting to the spirit. But any music that makes you conscious of all that is beautiful about you will be ideal. You may like to put the meditation on tape to guide you through your relaxation.

Lie on your bed and close your eyes. ... Become aware of yourself ... your body ... on the bed... in the room. ... Hear the music around you. Allow yourself to flow with the music. ... Now become aware of your breathing ... focus on your lungs as you breathe in ... and feel them expand. ... As you breathe out, feel your lungs contract ... breathe in ... breathe out. ... Be aware as you focus on your breathing how it becomes slower ... and deeper ... as you breathe in ... and out.

Now as you breathe in, allow the music to flow in on your breath ... in ... and out ... in ... and out. ... Let the music flow through you. ... Feel the music as the energy of love ... see its color, clear and pale when the music is gentle and slow ... more intense when the music is passionate ... increasing in depth of color as the music becomes even more passionate. ... And as the music and the colors flow through your body with each breath in ... and out ... in ... and out ... become aware of each part of your body as the music flows through it and around it.

As you breathe in, become aware of any tensions in your mind ... breathe out ... breathe in and direct your breath and the color of love to a point of fear or anger. ... Imagine the color of love absorbing that tension ... breathe out, knowing your breath and the love energy is taking the fear or anger with it, out of your consciousness.

As you breathe in, become aware of any tensions in your body ... breathe out ... breathe in and direct your breath and the color of love to a point of tension. ... Imagine the color of love absorbing that tension ... breathe out, knowing your breath and the love energy is taking the tension with it, out of your body.

As you breathe in ... and out ... in ... and out ... imagine the light of love flowing through your body and mind ... in ... and out ... unhindered ... uninhibited ... flowing around your body and mind as one entity ... enveloping you.

And now become aware of your breath ... become aware of the music ... breathe in ... and out ... in ... and out. ... Become aware of your body on the bed ... in the room. ... As your breathing normalizes, become aware of the room ... the spaces outside the room ... and become aware of the feeling in your body ... in your fingers ... your toes. ... And as you come back to the room ... to the present time ... and place ... be aware that — at any time — whenever it is needed, whenever you need to become calm, relaxed, and peaceful, the color of love can absorb and expel your fears, angers, and tensions of mind and body.

When you are fully present, open your eyes and sit up.

Yoga Sequence

The Mountain

The Mountain is a resting pose — return to it between poses to regain balance and stillness. It creates harmony in the body, aligns the body, improves posture, encourages body awareness, and stills the mind — all of which are necessary in creating a relaxed and attractive presence.

1. Stand with your feet 3 to 4 inches (9 to 11 cms) apart. Keep your weight evenly balanced on both feet. Move your weight slightly toward the outside of each foot, raising the arches.

2. Let your arms fall loosely at your sides and look straight ahead. Your head should be aligned with the spine, shoulders held back.

3. Relax into the position and be steady, still and tall — like a mountain. Make sure you are evenly balanced, and do not tighten the face muscles. Lengthen the spine and neck upward — this is a subtle movement but you will be able to perceive the sense of space it creates. You will suddenly feel much taller.

Variation

For an extra stretch, try raising your arms above your head with the fingers linked and palms facing upward.

Lengthen your whole body and if you can, lift your heels from the floor.

The Mountain

Variation

34

The Tree

The Tree calms the mind and soothes the nerves. It improves coordination and balance. It strengthens the legs and feet and lengthens the spinal column. Balance postures can be difficult for the beginner. However, the harmony of mind and body required can be quickly gained with concentration and perseverance.

1. While in the Mountain posture, fix your gaze on a spot on the wall in front of you. Keep looking at the spot throughout this posture, and maintain a slow and even breath.

2. Bend and raise one leg, so the sole of the foot is resting on the opposite thigh. You may need to use your hands to guide the foot into position. If you find raising one foot onto the thigh difficult, try placing it directly in front of the other foot — heel to toe.

3. Bring your hands into a prayer position. Try to achieve equilibrium, maintaining your gaze at the spot in front of you. If you lose your balance, lower the leg and begin again. If you are having difficulty, try focusing on a spot very close to you, or stand in front of a mirror. Keep the foot on the floor steady — do not let the foot or knee roll inward.

4. Once you can balance in the prayer position, try raising your arms above your head, palms touching. Stretch toward the sky.

Lower your arms to your sides, returning to the Mountain posture.

Step 3

Step 4

Remember to practice each pose on both sides — you may find one side easier than the other.

35

Chopping Wood

Chopping Wood releases stored tension and awakens energy in the body. It stimulates energy flow and tones the chest muscles.

1. From the Mountain posture, inhale, clasp your hands together and stretch your arms above your head. Stand with your feet directly aligned beneath your shoulders.

2. Exhaling strongly and in a single action, drop your upper torso down from the hips so your hands swing between your legs — do not bounce. Keep your arms straight.

Raise your arms and torso, then repeat the movement. Pretend you are chopping with an ax.

As you chop downward, let all tension or negative feelings be expelled from your body.

Come to rest in the Mountain pose.

Step 1

Step 2

Twisting Triangle

This twisting posture greatly enhances the flexibility of the hips. It is very refreshing, especially if performed quickly. It stimulates the nervous system, helps relieve depression and anxiety, tones abdominal organs, aids digestion, and increases flexibility.

1. Stand with your feet about 3 feet (1 m) apart, arms at shoulder height, in the Mountain pose.
2. Bending from the hips, lower your upper torso until it forms a right angle with your legs. Gaze straight ahead.
3. Swivel your torso, touching your left foot with your right hand. Your left arm should be straight. Look up at your left hand.
4. Now, twist to the other side to touch your right foot with your left hand.
5. Return to Step 2, where your body forms a right angle.
6. Raise your body back into the Mountain pose.
7. Repeat the whole process several times, either slowly or quickly.

Come to rest in the Mountain pose.

Step 2

Step 3

Massage

Massage is one of the great pleasures in which you can indulge. It is something you can share with your partner or you can do alone by visiting a professional massage therapist. If you are single and about to go out on a big date, a professional massage will be enjoyable as well as therapeutic.

Massage will ease all the stiffness in your muscles, leaving you feeling flexible physically and emotionally fluid — don't be surprised if you are in a daze for a little while after a good massage.

You can use oils to aid the movement of the hands over the skin. Oils also moisturize and soften the skin. Massage oils can be any good-quality, cold-pressed vegetable oil, though some are preferable to others. When essential oils are mixed into these "carrier oils" and massaged into the skin, their therapeutic properties are introduced into the body.

There are formal techniques you can use such as stroking, effleurage, frictions, petrissage, kneading, and percussion, but the techniques you develop at home can be relaxed, spontaneous and personal. Experiment, and work out what suits you and your partner.

A full body massage can be performed in any order. It is common to begin with the back including the shoulders, or back of the legs, progressing to the front of the legs, the arms, abdomen, and chest, and finishing with the neck and face.

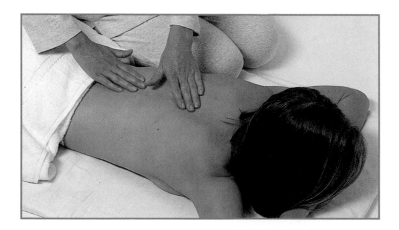

Getting Ready for the Big Date

So you've had a good run to drive out those nerves, you've immersed yourself in the deepest relaxation you've ever experienced, you've practiced some yoga and you've indulged in a massage and an aromabath. Now the time has come to dress for the evening.

You are no doubt walking on air by this time. Your skin and hair are glowing with health. Your expression is calm and your posture is straight. What you wear will reflect how you are feeling, so choose your outfit using your instincts, which are now heightened, rather than your intellect. And you will choose an outfit that will reflect you at your best.

Allow a couple of hours to dress, so you can take your time. Have a cup of herbal tea and listen to some music. Whatever you do, don't rush. Rushing will make you nervous, and you will lose the composure you've spent all the afternoon getting.

When the time comes to greet your date, you won't have to remember to smile, you just will.

Seduction with Scents

Scents are surer than sights and sounds
to make your heart strings crack.

Rudyard Kipling

Scents can have a powerful effect on our senses. They can influence our emotions and even our actions. Scent is highly individual and is perhaps the most potent seducer of all.

History has demonstrated that empires have been lost and gained through the influence of scents. The Queen of Sheba sought to seduce Solomon with fragrance. Cleopatra, as you will see when you read the story at the end of this book, perfumed the sails of her barge when she met Mark Antony for the first time.

It is important to realize, though, that not all scents work for all people. You must use your instincts to know which fragrances work for you. No matter how many people you know wear a perfume well, if you are not enraptured by it, chances are no one else will like it on you or around you either, so don't force it on yourself.

Sensual Scents
- Cinnamon
- Clary sage
- Frankincense
- Jasmine
- Myrtle
- Neroli
- Patchouli
- Rose
- Sandalwood
- Ylang-ylang

Aromabaths

This is a most luxurious indulgence and one that anyone can afford. It is comforting if you are tired or nervous, and especially if you are about to go out on a big date.

Essential oils, bubbles, candles, and music can all go toward the enjoyment of your bath. And know, too, that essential oils don't just work on a psychological level — they actually work on a physical level to calm your nerves, uplift your spirits, and increase your self-confidence.

Set up your bathroom with candles and music. Have big fluffy towels ready to drape yourself in once you step out of the bath, and one to roll up and put behind your head for comfort while you bathe.

Fill the bath with warm to hand-hot water and add 6 to 12 drops of up to three essential oils of your choice, or an already prepared combination for sensuality, just before getting in, and swish the water well to disperse the oils.

Lie in the bath for up to 30 minutes — allow your mind to wander and let your body relax until it feels light in the water.

Sensual Scents in the Bedroom

Your bedroom is where you need to feel as relaxed and as free in your spirit as possible.

When creating an atmosphere of sensuality, use candlelight. It creates soft light and is calming to the spirit, whereas harsh overhead lighting can create tension and disharmony.

Choose bed linen carefully. Many people prefer satin, but linen and fresh cotton are cool and comfortable, and their textures are stimulating to the skin. Keep your bedroom neat. Clutter creates an atmosphere of disharmony, and it collects allergy-inducing dust — sneezing and wheezing can ruin a romantic interlude. Colors are important, too, so refer to the chapter COLORS OF ATTRACTION on page 44 for ideas.

To fill your bedroom with subtle scent, use an aromatherapy burner. Burners are usually ceramic and come in a variety of colors and shapes. Some are electric, some attach to a light bulb, others use a candle inserted beneath the bowl to slowly heat the water containing the essential oils, which then gently scent the room.

Before a romantic evening, try out the oils to ensure they create the right atmosphere for you.

Colors of Attraction

*Woman begins by resisting a man's advances and
ends by blocking his retreat.*

Oscar Wilde

We, like the birds and animals in nature, use color in our rituals to attract a mate. We love color. Jewels are attractive to us because of the vividness and clarity of their color. Color is our first consideration when buying new clothes and accessories. And when we're choosing clothing and other adornments to make ourselves attractive to a potential lover, we take special care in our choice of color.

When you seek the advice of a friend on what to wear for your big date, you might ask: Does this color make me look sallow? Does it make me look fat? Does it bring out the color of my eyes? We always want to be sure that whatever we wear on that first date enhances the color of our eyes, because we know instinctively that our eyes are our most potent asset.

Color sets a tone. It lets people know how you are feeling, what personality type you might be, how healthy your self-esteem is, and what you expect from life. Colors can be gentle and soothing; they can be feminine, youthful, powerful, sensual, or erotic.

Your moods and your movements can be affected by color, even if that color is invisible to the world, beneath your outer clothing. Men and women are equally affected by the color and texture of their underwear: We all pay attention to the details when we are looking for someone special.

Color and Mood

Color affects your pleasure, so it is important for you to discover which colors bring out what moods. You need to know which colors make you feel sexy and which colors make you feel sensual, yet comfortable and relaxed. But most important of all, you need to know which color you associate with love.

Tuning into Love

Love seems to be a powerful feeling that comes and goes, something over which we have no control. But you can tune into love, making it an intense experience you can bring forth any time you wish, and color can be one of the most effective means of achieving this.

Sit quietly and let your mind float around thoughts of love. Let those thoughts become feelings without form. See if a sense of color emerges. It could be very faint at first, but if you gently focus on this feeling or sense, the color will become stronger and more intense. And as the color becomes more intense you will find that your experience of love will also grow stronger.

Feel this color, and feelings of love will radiate from you to others. Wear this color, and you will encourage romantic feelings your way. Practice visualizing this color and expand it to envelop you, especially when you feel insecure or lonely, and you will find that this is the color of your greatest comfort.

You can use this technique to discover which colors stimulate you and which colors calm you. Once you know the effect colors have on you, you will be able to alter your moods to increase positive feelings or to negate anger, hostility, or bitterness.

Use the colors that have positive effects on you in your clothing and in your home. Simply seeing those colors will lift your spirits and help center your being.

Your association of a color with a particular mood or feeling is a very personal thing, especially when it comes to the color that brings out the erotic in you or that heightens your sensuality. However, there are some standard ideas of what colors are erotic or sensual.

Erotic Colors

From most to least:

- Red orange
- Dark blue
- Violet
- Black
- Yellow
- Green
- Brown
- Gray

Sensual Colors

Especially in silks and satins:

- Pinks
- Ivory
- Greens
- Silver gray
- White
- Silver
- Soft gold

Generate Love with Crystals

*Love: The dirty trick nature played on us to achieve
the continuation of the species.*

W. Somerset Maugham

Many people believe that the crystals featured here emanate energies capable of helping us to give and receive love. Their influences are said to enhance our relationships by releasing blocked up feelings and balancing negative emotions.

Certain crystals are believed to act upon the heart chakra. This energy point is located in the center of the body at the level of the heart. It is the source of our love and is concerned with our sense of relationship: To ourselves, to others, and to our place in the world.

The right crystal for you is the one whose shape and color you find beautiful and for which you feel an affinity. Keep this crystal on your desk or near your bed. You may even like to sleep with one beneath your pillow.

Aventurine

Aventurine can be found in a variety of colors, including blue and reddish brown, but it is the cool green stone that we generally see.

A rejuvenating and soothing stone, aventurine assists us to accept and nurture ourselves. It is a crystal connected with feelings of contentment and joy and of being receptive and sincere. This crystal balances the male and the female energies within us and assists understanding in relationships between men and women.

Throughout history lovers have presented the objects of their desire with colorful stones as tokens of their love and esteem. They have served as marks of the wearer's sexual attractiveness and the giver's romantic heart.

Fluorite

Fluorite is usually a translucent white stone, but can be colored in the softest shades of pink, purple, green, and blue. Combinations of colors are often found with spectacular patterns and variations of color.

Fluorite calms the emotions and enables greater synergy between the rational and the emotional. Blue fluorite will cool the heat of anger; green and purple fluorite will induce us to more freely express love and affection; and clear fluorite will have a balancing effect, smoothing the transition from one emotion to the next.

Jade

Jade is found in white, brown, lavender, salmon pink, blue, yellow, and of course in every shade of green. In ancient China jade was believed to be pure water from the mountains that had crystallized. It was believed jade could generate vitality, good health, fertility, and wisdom within the one who owned it.

All colors of jade are beneficial to the heart. Blue jade has a calming quality and soothes the mind and the emotions. If anger and pent-up energy are restricting your actions, red jade can help relieve the tension by initiating the expression of these emotions. Lavender jade brings emotional balance, encourages the expression of unconditional love, and enables greater feelings of self-acceptance. Jade is a stone that elicits love, which can then be more easily and more readily expressed. Lavender and green jade balance the heart chakra.

Rose Quartz

Rose quartz has always been linked to the heart and love. It influences romantic love, love of self, and spiritual love. It increases your ability to receive love from another and opens the heart chakra to allow love to be more easily expressed. Color varies from a suggestion of pink to a translucent rose pink.

Rose quartz is said to awaken the eye and the soul to beauty. It also awakens the conscious mind to old emotional traumas, allowing them to be acknowledged and healed.

If you have a need for greater love or emotional healing, wear a piece of rose quartz as a pendant over your heart. This way, its influence is constantly present.

Lovers' Compatibility According to the Zodiac

A r i e s
The Ram
March 20 to April 20
Best Partner: Libra
Other compatible signs: Leo and
Sagittarius

G e m i n i
The Twins
May 20 to June 20
Best Partner: Sagittarius
Other compatible signs: Aquarius
and Libra

T a u r u s
The Bull
April 21 to May 19
Best Partner: Scorpio
Other compatible signs: Capricorn
and Virgo

C a n c e r
The Crab
June 21 to July 21
Best Partner: Capricorn
Other compatible signs: Pisces and
Scorpio

Leo
The Lion
July 22 to August 21
Best Partner: Aquarius
Other compatible signs: Aries and
Sagittarius

Virgo
The Virgin
August 22 to September 21
Best Partner: Pisces
Other compatible signs:
Capricorn and Taurus

Libra
The Scales
September 22 to October 22
Best Partner: Aries
Other compatible signs: Aquarius
and Gemini

Scorpio
The Scorpion
October 23 to November 21
Best Partner: Taurus
Other compatible signs: Pisces
and Cancer

Sagittarius
The Archer
November 22 to December 20
Best Partner: Gemini
Other compatible signs: Aries and
Leo

Capricorn
The Goat
December 21 to January 19
Best Partner: Cancer
Other compatible signs: Taurus
and Virgo

Aquarius
The Water-beater
January 20 to February 17
Best Partner: Leo
Other compatibles signs: Aries
and Sagittarius

Pisces
The Fish
February 18 to March 19
Best Partner: Virgo
Other compatible signs: Cancer
and Scorpio

Harmony and Happiness with Feng Shui

Omnia vincit Amor: et nos cedamus Amori.
Love conquers all: and we, too, yield to Love.

Virgil, *Eclogues*

If you are having problems in your relationship or love life, it could be because the chi (chee), or life force, is trapped, unable to flow smoothly about your home imparting health, happiness and prosperity. When the chi or life force is trapped, the energies in the environment become stagnant — and stagnant chi, according to the Chinese theory of feng shui, can cause disharmony within and between the people who inhabit that environment. On the other hand, energy that moves too quickly through your environment is in too much of a hurry to give you prosperity and good luck. The ideal is when the chi comes into your environment, moves slowly around, imparting health, happiness, and prosperity, before returning to nature and to heaven.

Feng shui (pronounced "foong swee" in Cantonese and "fong shwee" in Mandarin) means the flow of wind and water. The wind disperses chi, the invisible life energy, and the water contains it. Most people are affected by the atmosphere of a room. And the atmosphere of the room in which you and your partner sleep or spend most of your relaxation time can have a big impact on your level of relaxation and harmony.

The purpose of feng shui is to attract sheng chi (shung chee) or positive energy, and eliminate sha chi (shar chee), the negative or destructive energy. Sheng chi meanders along curved lines. Sharp angles or corners create "secret arrows" of negative sha chi that "attack" anyone in its path.

But there is no problem that can't be cured or, at the very least, improved. Cures range from altering physical structures and rearranging furniture to altering your perceptions with the use of wind chimes, crystals, mirrors, lighting, color, potted plants, and fish tanks containing goldfish.

Creating a Harmonious Flow of Energy in Your Home

Symmetry is one of the most important aspects of feng shui. If you have an L-shaped room, it is important to create two contained spaces, by using a screen, partition, or bookshelves. And

when it comes to choosing a crystal, an ornament, a potted plant, or a piece of furniture, be sure that its shape is balanced. Otherwise the chi may get trapped as it flows around your home and not be able to generate life-enhancing energy.

If a room feels too small or too large, or too hot or cold, color can alter its atmosphere considerably. Stand in the room. Take the time to allow your instincts to "sense" the effects that certain colors may have on the room. For instance, warm, pale colors could lift the energies in a small, cold room.

Rooms that are large and empty can make you feel as though your energies are being spread too thin. Large comfortable furniture, potted plants, and brightly colored woolen rugs could help contain your chi. But remember, feng shui is largely a matter of common sense and of allowing your instincts their say.

Some Feng Shui Cures

• Crystals are favorite feng shui cures. Hang them in the center of a window and they will draw chi into a room. Crystals must be symmetrical and faceted. Rough or animal shapes will not be effective.

• Indoor plants not only put life into a home, they are effective in hiding sharp corners that generate "secret arrows" of negative sha chi.

• Light should be soft in a bedroom. Natural light is good feng shui by day, and at night, table lamps and candles create soft light.

• Wind chimes deflect negative sha chi both inside and outside the home. Hang them in your bedroom and their song will ensure that you sleep peacefully. They also activate stagnant chi, so hang them in your bathroom.

The Bedroom

The bedroom is a place where you should feel at peace and completely secure. This is where you spend a third of your life, where you sleep, and where you are at your most vulnerable.

Your bedroom should be protected from the hot sun and from traffic noise. Facing east is suitable for the young, west for the elderly. If there is a bathroom attached, it should be well ventilated, otherwise stagnant chi will gather. Preferably, bedrooms should not be near the kitchen or storerooms because they too are potential sources of stagnant chi.

A low, slanting ceiling or beams over a bed direct negative sha chi which can cause headaches, illness, or confusion. An overhead beam that divides the bed of a couple can cause disagreement between them. Sharp corners on closets, dressing tables, bookshelves, doors, or the corners of irregularly shaped rooms will create "secret arrows" of sha chi. All corners should be covered, otherwise irritability or minor health problems could result.

The Bed

The most important aspect of good feng shui in the bedroom is the position of the bed.
• Diagonally opposite the door is the best place — this is the place of assembled chi. The area directly opposite or near the door is known as disturbed chi.
• A view of the door is good, but you should be some distance from it.
• If your head is in line with the bedroom door, you will be restless.
• The head of the bed should be against a solid wall.
• You should not sleep directly beneath a window. Make sure there is space for at least a small table or chair between you and the window.
• Chi can escape through the window at night, so make sure the curtains or blinds are closed.
• Make sure your bed isn't in a cross draft between the door and the window.
• Your feet should not be pointing toward the door. In many cultures, the dead are laid out with their feet pointing toward the door to allow their spirits easier access to heaven.

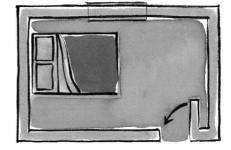

Looking for a Relationship

If you are having difficulty finding a relationship it may be you aren't paying enough attention to the yin or yang (depending on whether you are looking for a woman or a man) in your home. You can make adjustments to your decor to encourage someone to come into your life.

If you are looking for a man, you need to make the left (as you are facing the front of the house from outside) or yang side of your home eye-catching. By drawing attention to this dragon side of the house you are giving yourself the subliminal message you are attentive to men. There's no need to invest too heavily — flowers, paintings, or anything bright and cheerful will do. Take care you don't overdo it though — you may find you have more men than you can handle.

Of course, if you are looking for a woman you would brighten up the right side.

Making Amends

When you have had a serious argument with your spouse, tie your two wedding rings together with a red ribbon and put them on your bed head for seventy-two days. The love chi stored in the rings will heal the hurt each night while you lie in bed. If a couple is not married or doesn't have rings, they can tie two carved wooden turtles (which represent longevity) to the bed head.

Flowers — Messengers of Love

A fox is a wolf who sends flowers.

Ruth Weston, actress. Quoted in New York Post, Nov. 8, 1955

Since ancient times, particular flowers have been invested with romantic meanings. Lovers would send them to each other as coded messages. Flowers sometimes expressed feelings of love, or they were sent to discover the feelings of a coveted someone. This was a way to let a lover down gently, without him or her having to lose face. Sometimes, too, flowers were sent as warnings to a loved one — warnings of treachery, danger, or discovery.

Arum lily: great respect

Aster: change of heart

Baby's-breath: fertility

Buttercup: flirtation

Dahlia: treachery and danger

Daisy: innocence

Foxglove: trickery

Heather: betrothal

Honeysuckle: lovers entwined

Ivy: fertility and friendship

Jonquil: affection returned

Lilac: first love

Lotus (single): discovery of an illicit affair

Orange blossom: purity

Pansy: hopeful

Pink azalea: temperance

Pink rose: happy love

Red carnation: betrothal

Red chrysanthemum: I love you

Red pink: pure and ardent love

Red rose: love and romance

Red and white rose: unity

Rosemary: remembrance

Snowdrop: consolation

Tulip: perfect, eternal love

Violet: faithfulness

Wattle: sensitivity

White chrysanthemum: truth

White heather: good fortune

White rose: purity

White stock: lasting beauty

Yellow chrysanthemum: blighted love

Yellow crocus: symbol of Valentine's Day

Yellow rose: after argument adds insult to injury; under normal circumstances, a token.

Foods for Love

They dined on mince, and slices of quince,
Which they ate with a runcible spoon;
And hand in hand, on the edge of the sand,
They danced by the light of the moon.

Edward Lear, *The Owl and the Pussycat*

Food has long been associated with love. Both nourish the mind and body. Sharing food with someone you love promotes exquisite feelings of mutual warmth and generosity.

Any time of the day is good for sharing delectable foods with the one you love. Intimate breakfasts, picnics by a river, or a romantic dinner by candlelight — the choice is yours. The foods you choose should be light and easy to digest. Avoid difficult recipes — your mind should be on your lover, not on the mechanics of food preparation — but remember, tastes should be delicate and sensual. Use fresh ingredients that aid digestion, and do not repeat a flavor too often. Aim to make each course contrast and complement the ones before and following. For instance, try a spicy dish before something bland, or a creamy soup followed by a dry, crunchy dish. And avoid heavy sauces.

Setting the Scene

Creating atmosphere is very important, whether you are eating in your dining room or picnicking in a field. You do need to consider, however, that if you are eating out of doors, a wind may spring up, so you should prepare accordingly. Since it will be only you and your love, you can afford to use good china and your best silverware, even on a picnic. Perhaps you could leave the crystal glasses at home, but there are very nice glasses available for a low price that you could take instead.

When dining at home, the details of presentation need careful consideration. These are what will set the mood for the dinner. Set the table beautifully. Use a lovely tablecloth and napkins, fine china, crystal glasses, and your best silverware. An attractive wine bottle can be a decorative touch at the table, so look for interesting labels and bottle shapes. Fresh flowers are also an asset, but make sure that their perfume doesn't overwhelm the food and that their size doesn't keep you from making eye contact with your love.

Foods as Aphrodisiacs

In ancient civilizations and folk cultures, many herbs, fruits, and vegetables were regarded as promoting fertility. These often have distinctive shapes, such as corn, asparagus, carrots, avocados, and tomatoes, while at the same time have high nutritional values — fruits and grains literally contain the seeds of life.

It all began when Adam found an **apple** irresistible, thus sealing the fate of humankind. Apples were used in love divinations in folk cultures, and young girls will throw the peeled skin of an apple to discover the initial of their future husbands. According to the Classical poets Hesiodus and Alcaeus, the **artichoke** taken with wine incites wantonness and fleshly pleasure. Culpeper, the 17th-century English herbalist, declared that a decoction made from **asparagus** "... stirreth up bodily lust in man or woman, whatever some have written to the contrary." **Avocados** were believed by the Aztecs to stimulate passion, a belief shared by the court of Louis XIV in 17th-century France.

Bananas are among those fruits and vegetables credited by tribal peoples with aphrodisiac properties because of their phallic shapes. Young women were once courted in fields of **beans**, whose odor was said to drive them into a frenzy.

John Gerard the 16th century English herbalist, recommended **wild carrot** over the garden variety for "love matters," and **chervil**, according to Pliny, has the power to restore the spirits and refresh the body that "be overlaid and wearied with the use of women ..."

Fennel has a wide history as an aphrodisiac. Its use ranged from Egypt and the Mediterranean to the far northern reaches of Europe. A Hindu prescription for sexual vigor contains fennel juice, milk, honey, ghee, licorice, and sugar.

Some Aphrodiasiac Foods

Asparagus • Beans • Chocolate • Cream •
Fennel • Figs • Honey • Leeks • Licorice
• Onions • Peas • Pine nuts • Radishes •
Shellfish • Strawberries • Truffles

F i g s   also have a reputation in the East as a promoter of fertility. It is a Japanese custom to keep a potted fig tree to ensure a home of fertility and abundance. The ancient Greeks gorged on figs at the orgy of Dionysis in the belief they would aid their sexual prowess.

When the Roman emperor Augustus stayed with a man who was over a hundred years old and still fresh and lusty, he demanded the old man reveal the secret of his vigor. The man answered, "By using **h o n e y e d   w i n e** within, and oil without."

O n i o n s   have been known to have aphrodisiac qualities since the earliest times. In tribal South Africa, they are eaten during marriage ceremonies to increase the groom's virility. In medieval England, girls placed onions beneath their pillows to brings dreams of a future husband. **O y s t e r s** are regarded as the ultimate aphrodisiac. Casanova was so convinced of the power of the oyster, that he consumed 50 raw oysters every morning as he shared a bath with his lover of the moment.

P o m e g r a n a t e s   are an ancient symbol of fertility and abundance. Their powers have been praised throughout the Middle East and Asia, where they are sometimes included in marriage rituals to ensure fertility of the couple. **T o m a t o e s**   were nicknamed love apples, and **t r u f f l e s**   have a wide-ranging and long-held reputation as a powerful aphrodisiac. Madame du Barry and the Marquis de Sade praised the truffle as a prelude to lovemaking.

Romantic Dinner for Two

Menu

Shrimp in Champagne

Oysters on the Half-Shell

Fennel Soup

Fettuccine and Smoked Salmon

Avocado and White Grape Salad

Strawberries in Kirsch

Freshly Brewed Coffee

Wine Suggestions

Champagne makes the best aperitif and is an excellent accompaniment to the Shrimp. *Frascati*, a light Italian white wine goes well with the Fennel Soup.

Try *Chardonnay* with the Fettuccine and Smoked Salmon and with the Avocado and White Grape Salad.

With the Strawberries and Kirsch, choose a dessert wine such as *Rhine Riesling, Muscat,* or *Sauternes.*

The French always drink red wine with cheese — a good *Bordeaux*-style wine or a mature California red is ideal.

• Have an ice bucket ready for the champagne and check that there is ice in the freezer.

• Serve ice water to clear the palate between wines.

• Play low, romantic music (see MUSIC — THE LOVER'S GIFT on page 66.)

• At the end of the meal offer a selection of cheese and fresh figs, grapes and lychees presented on a beautiful platter.

• Aromatic, freshly brewed coffee completes the meal, perhaps served with chocolates.

Shrimp in Champagne

1 pound (455 g), (10 jumbo), cooked shrimp, peeled and deveined

2 tablespoons (50 g) butter

6 ounces (180 ml) brut champagne

1 medium onion, minced

1 medium clove of garlic, minced

2 tablespoons (50 g) fresh parsley, minced

juice of 1/2 lemon

1 teaspoon (5 ml) fresh tarragon, minced

Melt butter over a low to moderate flame. Add the onion, garlic, parsley, and tarragon. Sauté a few minutes until the onion is tender, not brown. Add the shrimp and lemon juice, toss to coat with butter mixture, and cook a few minutes to heat the shrimp through. Add the champagne. Set ablaze. The shrimp are ready to serve when the flames die down. Pierce with cocktail sticks before serving.

Oysters on the Half-Shell

Serve 6 raw oysters for each person. Present the oysters with a wedge of lemon and freshly ground black pepper. If you wish, you may also accompany the oysters with a shaker of hot red pepper sauce and a small dish of grated horseradish.

Fennel Soup

1 pound (500 g) of fennel bulb

1 tablespoon butter

1 small onion

6 ounces (180 g) boneless, skinless chicken breast

7 ounces (200 ml) dry white wine

1/4 teaspoon sugar

7 ounces (200 ml) chicken stock or broth

4 ounces (125 ml) fresh cream

1 tablespoon (25 ml) Pernod

Trim and discard the stalks from the fennel bulbs and cut lengthways into 1 cm (1/2 inch) slices. Using a sharp knife or scissors, finely cut fennel leaves, and set them aside. Cut the fennel bulb and onion in small slices and braise in butter in a heavy-based saucepan. Add chicken fillet and sauté without browning. Add dry white wine, sugar, and chicken stock, and simmer for 20 minutes until chicken and fennel are tender. Remove the chicken, finely slice, and set aside. Purée the cooked fennel and liquid in a food processor. Pour purée back into saucepan, add chicken, and reheat gently without boiling. Add the cream, Pernod, and add salt to taste. Stir well. To garnish, sprinkle some finely cut fennel leaves over the soup. Serve with croutons or toast.

Fettuccine and Smoked Salmon

4 ounces (125 g) plain fettuccine

4 ounces (125 g) spinach fettucine

4 ounces (125 g) smoked salmon, sliced

1 ounce (30 g) mushrooms, sliced

1 teaspoon (5 ml) chopped fresh parsley

1 chopped Spanish onion

1 teaspoon (5 ml) butter

1 garlic clove, minced

2 tablespoons (50 ml) low-fat sour cream

1 egg

salt and freshly ground black pepper

Heat the butter in a heavy skillet over low heat and sauté. Add the sliced mushrooms, onion, and garlic and sauté until soft. Whisk the egg with the cream, add salt and pepper to taste, then pour the mixture over the mushrooms and onion, mix well, and return to the heat, stirring constantly.

Put the pasta into 3 quarts of lightly salted boiling water and cook until tender. Drain in a sieve or colander. Put the cooked fettuccine and strips of smoked salmon into a bowl, pour the creamy mixture on top, and mix thoroughly with a fork and spoon. Garnish with fresh parsley and serve.

Avocado and White Grape Salad

1 large or 2 small avocados, peeled and sliced

2 tablespoons (50 ml) finely chopped shallots

½ lb (250 g) seedless white grapes

2 cups (500 ml) iceberg lettuce, torn into bite-size pieces

¾ cup (180 ml) extra virgin (first cold pressing) olive oil

1 tablespoon (25 ml) dry white wine

1 tablespoon (25 ml) vinegar

2 teaspoons (10 ml) Dijon mustard

1 clove garlic, minced or finely chopped

1 cup celery, cut into ½ inch (1 cm) pieces

salt and freshly ground black pepper to taste

Boston lettuce leaves for garnish

1 bunch watercress

a handful of cherry tomatoes

Stem the grapes. Wash and pat them dry. Chill. Combine the dry white wine, vinegar, mustard, salt, pepper, and garlic in a bottle, and shake until all thoroughly mixed. Mix avocado, grapes, mustard dressing, lettuce, and celery. Line a bowl or platter with Boston lettuce leaves. Spoon the salad into bowl or platter. Wash the watercress thoroughly and dry well. Place sprigs of watercress, alternating with cherry tomatoes, around the edge of the serving dish.

Strawberries in Kirsch

1 to 2 pints fresh strawberries, washed, hulled and sliced

2 to 4 tablespoons (50 to 100 ml) kirsch

1 teaspoon (5 g) superfine sugar

Place the sliced strawberries in a decorative bowl. Drizzle kirsch over the strawberries and refrigerate. Before serving, sprinkle sugar over the strawberries.

Music — The Lovers' Gift

It is cruel, you know, that music should be so beautiful.
It has the beauty of loneliness & of pain: of strength & freedom. The
beauty of disappointment & never-satisfied love.

Benjamin Britten, *Letters from a Life:*
Letters and Diaries of Benjamin Britten

Music has the power to transform and enrich your life. It can draw out hidden emotions, and make you sing with joy or cry with sorrow. It can inspire you and give you strength to undertake difficult enterprises. And it can soften the heart, allowing you to feel the grace of love.

The music on the following pages has been selected for lovers — much of it will reflect the various moods you experience with the one you love. A characteristic of the music by Chopin, for instance, is that his gentle, romantic melodies are suddenly interrupted by outbursts of great passion, their resolutions gentle and melodic. The lieder, which is poetry set to music, is very beautiful and gentle in nature, and very romantic. The operatic arias tend to be passionate, often involving yearning or lost love.

There is also a special section on music to help bring out feelings of anger and grief after a breakup. This music is often dramatic, often sad, often romantic, and beautiful. This music will help you let your broken heart express itself — a necessary indulgence for a period, because it enables you to recover quickly and in a healthy way.

Music is one of the greatest gifts of humankind. It comes in many forms, and can meet the needs of every conceivable mood or emotion. Take the time to experience music in a quiet environment, either alone or with the one you love, for it encourages us to express love in graceful ways. Listen to music with your beloved, for it can help draw your souls together as though they were one.

Piano

Scherzos by Chopin

Nocturnes by Chopin

Arabesque by Schumann

Three Pieces by Schubert

Moments Musicaux by Schubert

Impromptu Op. 90, No. 3 by Schubert

Fantasy in F minor for Four Hands by Schubert

Pathètique, Moonlight, and *Appassionata* Sonatas by Beethoven

Concertos

Piano Concertos Nos. 1 and 2 by Chopin

Piano Concerto No. 2 by Rachmaninoff

Rhapsody on a Theme of Paganini by Rachmaninoff (including 18th Variation)

Piano Concerto No. 1 by Grieg

Piano Concerto in A minor by Schumann

Piano Concerto No. 1 by Tchaikovsky

Cello Concerto in B minor, Op. 104, by Dvořák

Cello Concerto in E minor by Elgar

Variations for Cello and Orchestra by Max Bruch

Violin Concerto by Max Bruch

Slow movement, Clarinet Concerto in A by Mozart

Operas

Madama Butterfly by Puccini

La Bohème by Puccini

Tosca by Puccini

La Traviata by Verdi

Arias

"Maria" from *West Side Story* by Bernstein
"There's a Place for Us" from *West Side Story* by Bernstein
"La fleur que tu m'avais jetée" from *Carmen* by Bizet
"Au fond du temple saint" from *The Pearl Fishers* by Bizet
"Una furtiva lagrima" from *L'elisir d'amore* by Donizetti
"Recondita armonia" from *Tosca* by Puccini
"Ora stammi a sentir" from *Tosca* by Puccini
"E lucevan le stelle" from *Tosca* by Puccini
"Viene la sera" from *Madama Butterfly* by Puccini
"Un bel di" from *Madama Butterfly* by Puccini
"O soave fanciulla" from *La Bohème* by Puccini
"Un di felice" from *La Traviata* by Puccini
"Addio, al passato" from *La Traviata* by Puccini
"Parigi, o cara, noi lasceremo" from *La Traviata* by Puccini
"Hab mir's gelobt" from *Der Rosenkavalier* by Richard Strauss
"Tacea la notte placida" from *Il Trovatore* by Verdi
"Di tale amor che dirsi" from *Il Trovatore* by Verdi
"Gia nella notte densa" from *Otello* by Verdi
"Caro nome" from *Rigoletto* by Verdi

Song

Lieder by Schubert, Mendelssohn, Schumann, and Wolf
Songs by Grieg, Franck, and Fauré
Neapolitan songs
Four Last Songs by Richard Strauss

Orchestral

Daphnis et Chloe by Ravel
La Mer by Debussy
The Lark Ascending by Vaughan Williams

When a Relationship Ends...

"Dido's Lament" from *Dido and Aeneas* by Purcell
Slow movement, Symphony No. 7 by Beethoven
Pathètique, Moonlight, and *Appassionata* Sonatas by Beethoven
Piano Concerto No. 1 by Brahms
Etudes Op. 2, No. 1, and Op. 8, No. 12 by Scriabin
Slow movement, String Quartet No. 14 in
D minor ("Death and the Maiden") by Schubert
Nocturnes by Chopin
Ballades by Chopin
All concertos listed above
All operas and arias listed above

Love Spells

*To talk of honour in the mysteries of love, is like talking of Heaven or
the Deity in an operation of witchcraft, just when you are employing the
devil: it makes the charm impotent.*

William Wycherley, *The Country Wife*, Act 4

There's a little something in everyone that believes in the power of magic. Throughout the
ages, across the globe, from culture to culture, human beings have formulated spells and
potions to bring about good crops, good fortune, restoration of health, punishment of enemies,
and, most commonly of all, to win the love of someone dear.

The following are harmless spells that may encourage either your partner, or someone you
wish to become your partner, to hold a more loving attitude toward you.

Santería Love Spells

In Cuban and Puerto Rican *santería* (magic), love spells are the domain of the goddess Oshún,
the patron of gold and beauty. When properly addressed with a request for a love spell Oshún
is said to grant her devotees amorous adventures.

Spells from the balmy island of Cuba generally make use of flowers and herbs, and many
involve taking a bath to which a small amount of an infusion of different herbs has been
added. Love baths are used to imbue the user with the energies of attraction, and it is believed
that faithfully following the steps can result in meeting a wonderful new lover.

> The *botanicas*, or stores, selling Cuban and Puerto Rican magical
> herbs and religious goods are filled with a dazzling array of magical
> powders and oils for love spells. These are made in honor of the
> *santería* love goddess Oshún who is equated with Our Lady of
> Caridad del Cobre, also known as Our Lady of Charity.

A Cuban Love Bath

Acquire the following:

a large yellow candle

some cinnamon

honey

perfume

sugar

a few pinches of dried valerian root

Add the cinnamon, honey, perfume, sugar, and valerian root to a saucepan filled with water. Boil the mixture for 25 minutes, then set it aside to cool. Decant the strained mixture into a bottle with a lid, and add five coins of small denomination.

Draw a bath of warm water on a Friday evening, set the yellow candle next to it, and add a cupful of the infusion to the bath water. While you bathe visualize your aura as a golden light surrounding you. Envision yourself being the center of attention at a gathering of handsome men or beautiful women.

Blow out the candle and leave it where it is. The next night repeat the whole process, relighting the yellow candle. Continue for the next three nights until all the bath mixture is gone.

Wrap what remains of the candle in a piece of paper and put it in a safe place until you next wish to use it.

A Love Sprinkling Powder

Love powder can be clandestinely sprinkled on the belongings of a desired person and then in your own underwear drawer to forge a psychic love bond between you. This particular recipe is from the Caribbean and involves a number of herbs and oils.

To a handful of talcum powder add the following:

5 drops of rose oil

5 drops of sandalwood oil

7 drops of lavender oil

1 teaspoon of powdered cardamom seed

1 teaspoon of powdered allspice

1 teaspoon of crushed and dried lavender

1 teaspoon of crushed and dried rose petals

Mix all the ingredients together in a ceramic bowl with a fork. As you mix, visualize that a warm pink light is building and radiating out from the powder. Gently pour the powder into a little jar and take it with you to sprinkle on the belongings of the person you desire. Be sure to sprinkle a pinch of the powder on yourself every day after bathing.

Magical charms, powders, and oils will be most effective if they are created on a Friday, the sacred day of the planet Venus, the astrological patron of love.

This powder may also be used in a little charm to keep a friend or lover thinking about you while he or she is absent.

Place a small mound of the powder on the palm of your hand while standing in a sunny spot in a natural setting. Blow a little of the powder toward each of the four cardinal points (north, south, east, west), willing your beloved to feel the pull of your love and return soon.

A Bewitchment to Revive a Lusterless Relationship

The following spell makes use of crystals rather than herbs. You will need to take some of your lover's hairs from his or her hairbrush, a 4-inch (10-cm) square of red cotton or flannel, and a needle and red thread. You will also need a small piece of each of the following crystals:

aventurine   rose quartz   citrine

If for any reason you cannot obtain aventurine, use gold iron pyrites, also known as fool's gold.

Take the hairs obtained from the hairbrush and tie them to a few of your own, so that you have a small lock of hair knotted in the center. Place the lock of hair and the crystals in the center of the cotton or flannel and, if you like, add a few love herbs such as rose petals, orange blossoms, jasmine flowers, or any sweetly scented bloom.

Fold the cloth over the contents of your charm to make a small bag, then stitch the open edges to tightly seal the bag. Hold the bag in your hands and blow on it three times. Anoint the bag with a fragrant oil or perfume and envision it suffused in a glorious pink light.

Place the charm bag underneath the bed, now and then taking it out to reanoint it with your chosen perfume or essence.

Roses for Love

• A little rose water and honey in the rinse water of a lover's clothes
will promote loving thoughts when the clothes are worn.

• Freshly picked rose petals added to a bath full of water to
be shared by a couple are said to incite love and affection.

Two Great Love Stories

Tristan and Isolde

The greatest love stories involve sacrifice, yearnings, brief love, and loss. One of the Arthurian tales, Tristan and Isolde is the story of how Tristan's sense of honor and duty took precedence over his great love for Isolde, the result of which was great suffering for everyone concerned. One of the most loved stories of all time, the tale of Tristan and Isolde was made into an opera by Wagner.

When Arthur ruled Britain, a knight from Ireland arrived at the court of King Mark of Cornwall, demanding tribute. Tristan, the king's nephew, offered to fight the battle for Cornwall. Although he was wounded, Tristan inflicted injuries upon Moraunt so grievous that the Irish knight later died.

But Moraunt's lance was poisoned, and Tristan became ill. He set sail for help in another kingdom, but his boat was driven by storms to Ireland. The king of Ireland and his daughter Isolde saw Tristan playing his lute on the beach and sent for him. Tristan kept his identity secret, and while Isolde nursed him, they fell in love. When he was restored to health, it was discovered that it was Tristan who had killed Moraunt, the queen's brother. The queen demanded vengeance but the court declared that he be sent home never to return.

King Mark became intrigued by Tristan's descriptions of Isolde the Fair. He ordered his nephew back to Ireland to obtain Isolde to be his queen. With a heavy heart, but bound by his oath, Tristan embarked for Ireland.

Again thrown off course by storms, Tristan found himself at Camelot. The King of Ireland was facing charges of treason against Arthur. Tristan helped clear the Irish king. In gratitude, the king offered Tristan any boon. With a trembling voice, Tristan demanded Isolde for his uncle, the king of Cornwall.

The queen asked Isolde's maid to administer a love potion to Isolde and Mark, but on the ship, the maid gave Isolde and Tristan the love potion instead.

Isolde the Fair and King Mark were married, but in an act of knightly honor, Mark lost Isolde to the Saracen knight, Sir Palamedes. Tristan recovered Isolde for the king, but before he restored her to Mark, they lived in the forest for a short time. Mark was full of jealousy and nearly killed Tristan. He banished Tristan and locked Isolde up in a tower.

Time went by, then Tristan aided King Hoel of Brittany in a war. In gratitude, Hoel offered Tristan his daughter, Isolde of the White Hands, in marriage. Tristan's love for Isolde the Fair was hopeless, and it seemed as though destiny had provided Isolde of the White Hands only for his happiness. After a time, war broke out again and Tristan was severely injured. His wife tried to cure him, but Tristan became weaker. He asked his wife to send for Isolde the Fair, since her ministrations had cured him in the past. Isolde of the White Hands agreed and Tristan asked the servant that if the queen of Cornwall returned with him to put up white sails; that if she had refused, black sails.

When Isolde of the White Hands learned of the previous love between Tristan and the queen of Cornwall, she directed that Tristan be told the returning ship bore black sails. In grief, Tristan died. Isolde the Fair arrived too late to save Tristan; she died holding him. Their bodies were returned to Cornwall, where King Mark, full of sorrow, had them buried side by side with a vine on Tristan's grave and a rose on Isolde's. The plants grew inextricably intertwined.

Antony and Cleopatra

The love affair between Antony and Cleopatra is one of the world's greatest romances, one upon which the fate of an empire hung and one that has reverberated through 2,000 years of poetry and song. It took place between 41 and 30 B.C., against the backdrop of the expanionist forces of the Roman Empire.

When Cleopatra was 21 years old, Julius Caesar was so entranced by her that he set her upon the throne of Egypt. Cleopatra was beautiful and bewitching, charming all who met her.

After Caesar's assassination three years later, the Roman Empire came under the dual control of Mark Antony and Caesar's heir, Octavian. Antony was described as having the noble and masculine appearance of Hercules. He was flamboyant, generous, and a courageous and energetic general. At the time of his meeting with Cleopatra, he was 42 and she was 28.

Antony had summoned her several times to Cilicia to answer an accusation against her. For a time, she ignored Antony's summons. Then one fine day, she sailed up the river Cydnus in a gilded barge with purple sails, and oars of silver that beat time to flutes and harps. Cleopatra, attired as Venus, reclined under a canopy of gold. She was attended by boys dressed as cupids and maids dressed as nereids and graces. Fragrances drifted from the barge's sails to the riverbanks crowded with citizens. The city of Tarsus was empty, except for Antony sitting upon the tribunal awaiting her.

Cleopatra was beautiful, theatrical, and wily in love. She matched Antony's every mood and never let him out of her sight, day or night. She played dice with him, drank with him, hunted with him, and even watched him as he practiced his skills in arms.

Antony gave Cleopatra kingdom after kingdom — in Phoenicia, Syria, Cyprus, Turkey, Judea, and Arabia. They named their twin children Alexander and Cleopatra, adding to their names the titles Sun and Moon.

During this time, Antony was married to Octavian's sister Octavia, and they also had children together. Although Antony and Octavia's marriage was merely a political alliance, the Roman people resented the way Antony flaunted Cleopatra. His love for Cleopatra increasingly distracted him from the affairs of Empire, and the Romans became alarmed by his military neglect and failures.

In 32 B.C., Octavian persuaded the Senate to revoke Antony's commission to govern the Eastern Empire and to declare war on Cleopatra. The campaign was disastrous for the lovers, and by 30 B.C., Antony's land and sea forces deserted him for Octavian.

Antony was convinced Cleopatra had betrayed him to Octavian. He returned to Alexandria, accusing Cleopatra. She fled to a monument that she used as her treasury, and locking herself in, she sent word to Antony that she was dead. Antony cried out: "I shall soon be with you!" and fell on his sword. He did not die immediately, however, and Cleopatra had him brought to her. She laid him on a bed and he died in her arms. Plutarch described the scene: "Those that were present say that nothing was ever more sad than this spectacle, to see Antony, covered all over with blood and just expiring, thus drawn up, still holding up his hands to her, and lifting up his body with the little force he had left."

Worried that she would destroy the wealth of Egypt, Octavian attempted to make a treaty with her, but she wanted nothing but to be buried in the same tomb as Antony. She killed herself by embracing an asp that had been smuggled to her in a bowl of figs.

Index

TIME-LIFE BOOKS IS A DIVISION OF TIME LIFE INC.

TIME-LIFE CUSTOM PUBLISHING

Vice President and Publisher	Terry Newell
Associate Publisher	Teresa Hartnett
Vice President of Sales and Marketing	Neil Levin
Director of New Product Development	Quentin McAndrew
Director of Special Sales	Liz Ziehl
Project Manager	Teresa Graham

TIME-LIFE is a trademark of Time Warner Inc. U.S.A.

ISBN 0-7835-5257-2
CIP data available upon application:
Librarian
Time-Life Books
2000 Duke Street
Alexandria, VA 22314

Printed in Singapore by Tien Wah Press (Pte) Ltd

With thanks to Matthew Green for his contribution to the spells chapter.